The Trees of Life

A Scriptures Summary

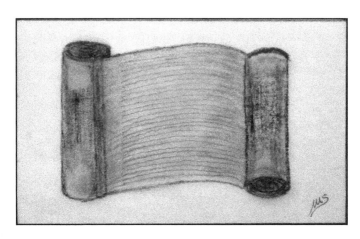

From Genesis to Revelation

MARIO SOSTIZZO

ISBN 978-1-63844-266-0 (paperback)
ISBN 978-1-63844-267-7 (digital)

Christian Faith Publishing, Inc.
832 Park Avenue
Meadville, PA 16335
www.christianfaithpublishing.com

Printed in the United States of America

Dedicated to my grandchildren—someone came to conclude:
"I guess reading the scriptures makes you live longer."

Contents

Introduction... 9
Meaning: Historic (H), Prophetic (P), Didactic (D)

Old Scriptures 11

    Book 1:   Genesis (H).................................. 13
    Book 2:   Exodus (H) 15
    Book 3:   Leviticus (H).................................. 16
    Book 4:   Numbers (H) 17
    Book 5:   Deuteronomy (H)........................... 18
    Book 6:   Joshua (H) 19
    Book 7:   Judges (H) 20
    Book 8:   Ruth (H) 21
    Book 9–10: Samuel 1 and 2 (H) 22
    Book 11–12: Kings 1 and 2 (H)...................... 23
    Book 13–14: Chronicles 1 and 2 (H) 25
    Book 15:   Ezra (H).. 26
    Book 16:   Nehemiah (H) 28
    Book 17:   Esther (H)..................................... 29
    Book 18:   Job (D) 30
    Book 19:   Psalms (D) 31
    Book 20:   Proverbs (D) 32
    Book 21:   Ecclesiastes (D) 33
    Book 22:   Song of Songs (D)........................... 34
    Book 23:   Isaiah (P) 35
    Book 24:   Jeremiah (P) 36

Book 25: Lamentations (P) 37
Book 26: Ezekiel (P) 38
Book 27: Daniel (P) 39
Book 28: Hosea (P) 40
Book 29: Joel (P) 41
Book 30: Amos (P) 42
Book 31: Obadiah (P) 43
Book 32: Jonah (P) 44
Book 33: Micah (P) 45
Book 34: Nahum (P) 46
Book 35: Habakkuk (P) 47
Book 36: Zephaniah (P) 48
Book 37: Haggai (P) 49
Book 38: Zechariah (P) 50
Book 39: Malachi (P) 51

Covenant between God and People: The Ten
    Commandments.................................... 52
Prophets: Visionaries, Dreamers, Predictors 53

New Scriptures 55

Book 1: ˈMatthew (H) 57
Book 2: Mark (H) 60
Book 3: Luke (H)... 63
Book 4: John (H) 65
Book 5: Acts of the Apostles (H) 67
Book 6: Romans (D)..................................... 70
Book 7–8: Corinthians 1 and 2 (D) 72
Book 9: Galatians (D) 74
Book 10: Ephesians (D) 75
Book 11: Philippians (D) 76
Book 12: Colossians (D) 77

Book 13–14: Thessalonians 1 and 2 (D) 78
Book 15–16: Timothy 1 and 2 (D) 80
Book 17:   Titus (D) 82
Book 18:   Philemon (D) 83
Book 19:   Hebrews (D) 84
Book 20:   Thiago (D) 86
Book 21–22: Peter 1 and 2 (P) 87
Book 23–25: John 1, 2, and 3 (P) 89
Book 26:   Jude (P) 91
Book 27:   Revelation (P) 92

Statements 95
Prayer 97
Chronological Events 99
References 101
Index 103
By the Author 105
About the Author 106

Introduction

This historical summary of the millennial's scriptures, telling in the simplest manner, makes the readers open the interesting door for the knowledge of the humanity development.

The Scripture is a collection of books written in diverse periods, by diverse authors, and in diverse literary genre. There is no scientific guaranty that everything in the Scripture is solid religion teaching because it includes traditions, interpretations, and revelations.

These books were assembled, and the first five historical books of the Old Scriptures, are about the Old Covenanted agreement between God and the Jewish people.

The Old Scriptures are seventeen historical books including these five about the Covenant period from Moses, including five didactic books that are about the knowledge and the feelings of the people. The prophetic books are seventeen and bring the message of the prophets; all making thirty-nine books.

At the New Scriptures are twenty-seven books founded in the full life of Jesus Christ and written by the apostles. The first five books are historical followed by fifteen didactic books and the last seven prophetic books.

Old Scriptures

We can't start by telling the Old Scripture's history, even in a compact way, without telling about the center control of the Roman Empire which was *Rome*, the eternal city with greatly established *religion, politics,* and *commercial center.* It was a city founded in 753 BC, the beginning of an empire which fell in AD 476.

So in the middle of this period, the old scriptures and the new scriptures were divided under the Roman Emperors, Julius Caesar and Augustus (in which time was born Jesus Christ) and then after with Nero, Vespasian, and Titus (not friends of the Christians), until the day the Emperor Constantine released the Christian religion.

In today's Israel, *the city of Jerusalem is the center* of the Judaism culture, but nearby it, at the Mediterranean Sea border, is the city of Caesarea (today's Tel Aviv) from where the ships that were the linkage of Jerusalem and Rome arrive and depart—a much different culture.

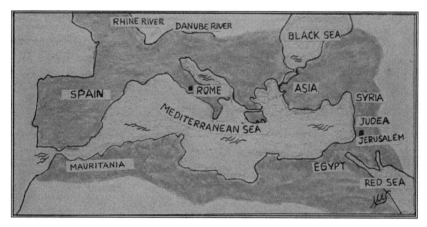

Roman Empire

Book 1

Genesis

The beginning; the history by word-of-mouth; the starting book. It tells the beginning of the universe, as well the humanity, civilization, and Judaism nation. *Abraham* lived at least from 700 to 1,000 years before Moses, but he wrote at least five books of the Old Scriptures, till the Abraham grandson, Joseph, which lived around 1800 BC. *The collection* was assembled when kings were leading Israel.

At the beginning, theoretically, the humanity developed in the Garden of Eden. It was a place between the Euphrates and the Tigris Rivers, which runs to Persian Gulf—to the north was the city of Haran, at the center was the city of Babylon, and in the south was the city of Ur, the homeland of Abraham.

Descendants of Abraham moved and settled in the Canaan region of Israel, but a seven-year drought made them abandon the region and go to Egypt that had abundant water from the Nile. At that time, Jacob with his son, Joseph, who was Pharaoh's friend, accepted to go to Egypt, going by the coastal way.

So after more than four hundred years, the descendants of Jacob were a foreign people who were still living there, initially out of invitation but after, by the *changes of Pharaohs, the latter enslaved them.* About this time, the lands of Canaan were taken by the Philistines.[1]

---

[1] Philistines—these people from the north of Israel, perhaps from Greek islands, came to the coast and stayed at the same time the Jews were in Egypt; they stayed there, fighting for the land until they became part of that continent region.

Book 2

Exodus

God's *messenger* sent Moses to free them from slavery. To help him, the God of *Moses*, in order to convince the god Pharaoh, sent ten catastrophic plagues to allow the Israelites to leave Egypt and go back by the desert way of Sinai mountains. Camping at these mountains, God gave to Moses the *Ten Commandments* which they should practice for the life of their culture in the promised land. The stone table carved with the Ten Commandments was later placed in an ark which they called the Ark of the Covenant between Jews and God.

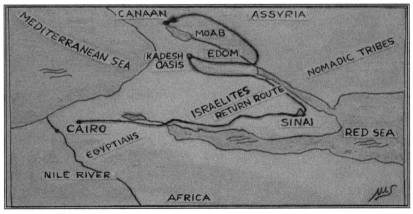

Exodus—Returning from Egypt

Book 3

Leviticus

This is the *history* book that explains how to live in God's presence. It isn't known who wrote this book but the writing of this book was determined to be at about 1450 BC. At that time, the book was known as the *Priest's* Manual.

At that time also, *sheep and lambs* were *worshiped*,[2] the rich people till bulls, but the poor the little birds—everything to get the mercy for the sins in respect to God and be purified.

---

[2] Jewish stopped to worship animals after the Romans destroyed their temple in Jerusalem by the years AD 40 thru 70.

Book 4

Numbers

Then *Moses's* writing *history* with his people, after one year *camped in the Mount Sinai*, "decided to make a census" with decision to take back the land of Canaan, the promised land, but they couldn't take over that land from the people that was living there at that time, so they camped for forty years at two hundred kilometers far, in the region of Edom in the east side of the Jordan River.

Book 5

Deuteronomy

Deuteronomy means "the repetition of law."

Continuing to write about his people's *historical* adventure—*Moses* was already one hundred twenty years old by that time. He made another census and decided to go back to the promised land of Canaan, but *Moses died during the trip* before he reviewed the *messages and directions* from God to him and his people, leaving Joshua as his leader. This way, the five books during the life of Moses were completed.

Joshua invaded Canaan, and the people received the promised land back. Recognize in your heart, the same way a man teaches his son, so the Lord your God have instructed you, to keep His Commandments[3] for the respect to the others, the nonreciprocity to the evil, the love as basics from the family to the people. Rise like rain my teaching, spread like the dew my words, like downpour to the grass, and like drops over the veggies.

---

[3] Many of the laws were left to the Jews, only were abandoned, by the Good News, taught by Jesus Christ, mainly the end of the sacrifices to pay for the sins.

Book 6

Joshua

The *mission* that *Joshua* received put him in a responsible position to complete the return to the holy promised land. The repossession happened around 1200 BC; all the twelve tribes of Israelites spread to the Canaan land as set before by Moses. Israel exist again. Joshua lived till one hundred and ten years old, have completed his mission.

Book 7

Judges

Judges—title for a tribal leader.

The book was written by the time of King David and includes *history* that happened on Jordan River and Israel land. Circa 1000 BC—*King David* was expanding territory, taking over on Jerusalem, and transforming it as Israel's capital with the help of the judges (leaders). One of the most known leaders who lived in his time was *Samson* who killed 1,000 Philistines with a donkey's jawbone. But he fell to a trap by the Philistine Delilah "who cut his long hair, which he was keeping to provide strength" as he promised to God.

Book 8

Ruth

Ruth *was the great-grandmother of King David.* She married Boaz, "had a son Obed" who was to be the father of Isai, the father of David, descending to Jesus centuries later. *Ruth* lived around 1100 BC. The *history* book was from Solomon's time.

 # Books 9–10

Samuel 1 and 2

The books were written around 1000 BC. *Samuel,* at the beginning, was a spiritual and political *leader*, was a judge to solve disputes. By this time David was a young pastor who *"fought and defeated Goliath,"* a strong Philistine. The *Ark of the Covenant* was used in battles to repossess the holy land, Israel, from the Philistines.[4] Much later, "David with 30 years old, rises to be King of Judah" and Jerusalem, so, "all Israel. *David reign about 40 years,"* about 1000 years BC. His tough was to transform Jerusalem into the spiritual and political center of Israel.

---

[4] Descendants of the *Philistines, now the Palestinians*, were those established in the Gaza Strip.

Books 11–12

Kings 1 and 2

Was to *Solomon* the duty to build *Israel's first religion temple*, which until then was called a tabernacle tent. The temple was constructed in about seven years and has taken two hundred thousand soldiers from the military work resources. In the next 450 years, Judah, with Jerusalem as capital, separated from the Northern Israel, and each region had its king.

Solomon started to expand territory, his one thousand wives, gave problems, intrigues and idolatry. Was created religion *conflicts and idolatry worship were practiced*, as well due to the influence of the wives, with fights between the descendants. Living in idolatry and sin, God abandon them. It was during Solomon's time in around 950 BC. The Assyrians[5] destroyed the north of Israel in 700 BC—in this period, there were nineteen kings. After that, the Babylonians[6] destroyed the south of Judah in about 600 BC—during this time, there were twenty kings—and the Jews who *survived were exiled in Babylon* (which

---

[5] Assyrians—They lived in the east of the Israelites' lands and invasions to get tax possessions were the cause for constant war between the kings.

[6] Babylonians—They lived at the east of the Assyrians. When the Assyrians lost power with so many battles, the Babylonians took over them and reached Israel, destroying what was remaining of the Israelites.

is Bagdad, Iraq, today), more than 1,500 kilometers far. That time the books were written, Jews were precise in recording *history*. Till that, the Persians[7] were superiors for the Babylonians, and the Jews returned to their homeland.

---

[7] Persians—This civilization was living in the seacoast, which has its name, Persian Sea. Their domination was from the third century BC to the second century AD, wherein their only rivals were the Romans and Greeks.

Books 13–14

Chronicles 1 and 2

In these books are recorded David's preparation for the construction of the Jerusalem Temple by his son *Solomon. The first book, starting from Adam and Eve and their descendants, listed two thousand names, Abraham being the hundredth.* With this, summarizing the links of David's families and leaders, it was recorded *history* showing the lineage in face to God. But on the second book is found the bad things Solomon and his successors did, up to the exile of Jews for fifty years in Babylon, confirming the power and *promises by God's covenant* with regard to the promised land. In regard to the religion sins, God's covenant should never be left but have done renewed believes in Him.

The south region, Judah, was more religious and compromised with God, but the north region believes in idols and had sinner kings. That way came the prophets, which provided advices to the north region about the bad things that could happen in their way. And then came one of the more known prophets, *Isaiah, who was taking the word of God, advising the Jewish nation about the consequences of the wrong things.*

Book 15

Ezra

This Old Scriptures book was written by *Ezra,* and elapsed approximately one hundred years. *The rabbi, Ezra, came up to give direction to Jewish faith,* bringing the people to accomplish the covenanted commandments with God, including taking the rules against idolatry. This way, some adjustments had to be done because radical old rules came back and it was already rules on the past, like the Jewish men marrying with non-Jewish, which included according to the priests, the idolatry that brought bad luck to Israel.

By around 500 BC, the return of the Israelites was only possible because of the power of the Persian Empire that came to dominate over Babylonians, Assyrians, and Israelites. They continued at Africa's side, up to Egypt and Libya, resulting in a second chance to rebuild Israel. The Persians based in Iran, allowed freedom to 42,000 Jews back to their land, and helped them to rebuild their temple, providing most of the resources including what was stolen by the Babylonians.

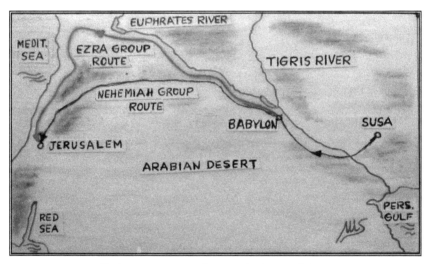

Exile—Returning from Babylon and Susa

Book 16

Nehemiah

He was a Jew who worked with the Persian King and knew Ezra. He convinced the king to help Israel rebuild the Babylonian wall's destruction.

Nehemiah's book is the *history* about departing from Susa, capital of the Persian Empire, and going to Jerusalem with the work power of two thousand soldiers, and the citizen of Jerusalem rebuilding the wall around Jerusalem in fifty-two days. Ezra attributed the achievement to God's help, the freedom and reconstruction after fifty years in exile.

Book 17

Esther

It is not known if the book was written by *Ezra or Nehemiah* and is uncertain about if it was some *story* event or one invented by storytellers. It happened in the capital, Susa, of Iran, today: Shush. Esther complied the king's contest for a vacant queen position and won the king's attention. As the wife of the Persian King, Xerxes, for twenty years, Esther did influence the *return of Jewish people from exile*. Since Esther was Jewish, her story was important to be part of the scriptures.

Book 18

Job

Lived in the time of Abraham at around 2000 BC. It is the *history* saying that to the good *Job* there happened a lot of bad things till nothing had remained—not his wealth, herds, health, and his ten children and family. By his faith, he never cursed God about this bad luck. Then Job had a talk with God, with complains, to *understand the meaning of life,* and so he could rise from the ashes. He understood his destiny, returned to the second part of his life, and lived one hundred forty years of age, "giving to him other ten children which were taken before, he saw his greats-grandchildren living."

Book 19

Psalms

Are phrases, *prayers*, songs praising God during religious worship by *Jews* in the temple, like marriage, king's coronation, and religious days.

A lot of Psalms were referenced to David, some to Solomon, others inspired by Moses, while much happened in exile times in Babylon or in Egypt. These *writings were in lamb skin rolls* and have origin in the 1400 BC till 500 BC. The psalms translated thanksgiving, request for help, complaining, favors, sorrow of the Jews to God. The *David* Psalms assembled five books of songs and are hymns reverencing God.

Lord you have been our refuge from generation to generation, before the mountains created, the earth and the world had formed, because thousand years to your eyes, are like yesterday that passed overnight and so the years without estimation.

Book 20

Proverbs

Writings with origins in the time of *Solomon* in 900 BC. But a lot of the proverbs have origin from *writings* in Egypt four hundred years before, *made by old people to teach the younger*—living experiences, luck and lost, behavior, advices, relationship, marriage, having family, negotiations, and religion. The proverbs have one or two lines (e.g., "Take this opportunity, remember at the river that water passes only once," "Do not forget you will be harvesting what you are planting," and "A defaming gossips can destroy the best friend's relationship").

Book 21

Ecclesiastes

Attributed to *Solomon*—the most intelligent king of Israel. He questioned, *"What is the meaning of the human's life?"* This book, *rewritten* in 400 BC, records how the logics are explored, how the people measure its values by the work, accumulated riches, wisdom, acquired education, achieved pleasures, friendship, and relationships.

"Under the Sun I worked hard to leave to an heir, wise or foolish, deserving or not." Couldn't reach to a conclusion, as well as with this example, a couple was mourning his child, but an elder simple person that never did some remarkable, for some reason, was dying old—how much injustice. And then the conclusion that he got was, "Fear God and will be blessed and happy at end of your life." We are a shade of the sun, arrived, and like the wind, we leave this existence, and with time, we are forgotten.

Book 22

Song of Songs

Songs attributed to *Solomon's* times—*praising the relationship* between a man and a woman, picking the fruit from *the trees of life.* The songs were understood as symbolic love or compliments between a couple and, in a much higher level, the spiritual love *between God and each one of us.*

Book 23

Isaiah

With him, God passed the *message* that by continuously living as sinners, Israel would be destroyed, which did not happen with Moses's covenant. But he was going to have a new beginning, and he will send a *Messiah Savior, descending from King David,* establishing a great kingdom never imagined by the Jews.

Isaiah with this *prophecy,* wrote this book, but later on, other Jewish prophets extended more chapters to include the time of the Babylon exile and freedom from there, and the name of the Persian King, Cyrus, was found in the book. This way, this book was written from 700 BC till 400 BC.[8] when the Jews had Israel again.

---

[8] Later on at the New Scriptures, Isaiah was well-known as the fifth gospel. Matthew—Marcos, Lucas, John, and Isaiah. Isaiah previewed the birth, life, and condemnation of Jesus, the Messiah Ismael.

Book 24

Jeremiah

He already knew about the Assyrian invasion one hundred years before and *predicted the invasion of the Babylonians* in 600 BC. *Jeremiah*, in the exile, during the battle, advised the Jewish king to surrender. This saved him and allowed him to rewrite his book, after the king have burned its history and *prophecies* scroll. To be prophet in that time was a hard mission—preaching God's existence, supporting the Jewish believers, going against sin (e.g., idolatry), advising the wrong behavior of sacrifices, predicting the major catastrophes of their kingdom.

One of God's messages to Jeremiah used a potter's shop example on doing the pots, *As the potter have the clay in his hands, so are you in my hands.* At that time, making pots was a big business and done with the potter's hands like today. If the pots was not coming the way the potter wants it, he remakes the clay and starts over again in a better shape.

Book 25

Lamentations

Translated in words, the pain suffered with almost the extermination of the people and the destruction of stone over stone of Jerusalem, by the Babylonians invasion, made all Jewish *songs* of this event are lamentations because of Kings sword came over them, old or young, boys and girls, killed by the enemy. The writer of the lamentations is the prophet *Jeremiah, invocating God's mercy to sinners or giving thanks* for have not been completely exterminated.

Book 26

Ezekiel

Also a writer from exile. for all the Jewish that made a community live exiled in the Babylonian region, today called Iraq.

Ezekiel was initially a rabbi in Jerusalem, but the people promoted him to be prophet. The most famous *vision* of Ezekiel was at a valley with human skeletons. In a sequence of actions with the wind, the skeletons assembled together, got flesh, and resurrected—it was *a message from God* on what was going to be done with the Jewish nation, returning to existence. Another important *vision* was when he saw God approaching him—a *four-winged creature pulling a chariot with God's throne*. This was symbolically interpreted to be in the future, the four evangelists/writers of Christ's gospels—Mark being the Lion, Luke the bull, John the eagle, and Matthew as the human face.

Book 27

Daniel

When he was twenty years of age, he was kept prisoner with others Jews and exiled by the Babylonians. *Daniel* was a prince of a good sense, was chosen to assist the Babylonian king, showed *qualities of interpreting dreams and prophetic visions.* The King speaking to Daniel, are you one of the captives son of Judah, that came with my father? I have heard that you have the God's spirit and you show to have a superior level of science, intelligence and knowledge.

With the King Nebuchadnezzar's dreams, Daniel showed the power to *interpret* his dreams, predicting the fall of the Babylon Empire to the Persians at around the 600 BC. He worked sixty years in Babylon (what is now Iraq); several *visions* were interpreted in detail, including Angel Gabriel explaining to Daniel God's messages—the most relevant one of which was the vision of the four beasts—lion, bear, leopard, and a creature—in reference to four powerful kingdoms of the world at that time that should battle with the neighbors for territory. When the Persians invaded and smashed the Babylonians, the Persian king noticed the then old Daniel's qualities and made him also his valued advisor and administrator in Persia (modern Iran).

Book 28

Hosea

He is a dreamer and *vision* interpreter like others small prophets. Among his small books, Isaiah, Jeremiah, Ezekiel, and Daniel were the great and most important ones. From Isaiah circa 700 BC till Malachi circa 400 BC, according to *Hosea*, he tells all, and *the list of sins of the Jewish was long*—idolatry, lies, theft, adultery, violence, murder, sacrifices, prostitution, and sex in the temples looking for fertility, been for agriculture and making raining. Hosea, in *his dreams*, listened to God commanding him to marry a prostitute, to understand the relationship he wanted from the Jews, understanding and reconciliation. The prophet anticipated the destruction by the Assyrians and Babylonians, the exile of the remaining, the purification of their souls, and the return to the teaching of Moses, with the covenant done with God.

Book 29

Joel

Like a small prophet, he describes *his visions* about grasshopper's invasion, a frequent swarm coming from the desert and destroying the agriculture and everything ahead. This way, *the interpretation was in relation to the neighbor's invasion,*[9] coming from above the Jerusalem walls. *Joel* requested to the people to repent of the sins and have fear of God, considering all the sins that he was seen around himself. A large part practicing—idolatry, exploiting the poor, buying justice in the courts for offerings.

---

[9] The invasions were done by the Assyrians, Babylonians, Persians, and Greeks.

Book 30

Amos

A poor prophet, who as a boy was following his mother in begging for help. He was a shepherd when *his visions* happened circa 800 BC. He was taking care of a farm of sycamore when he walked up from south of Jerusalem to the north of Israel in Samaria to tell the messages received from God in his visions. *Amos's* visions were about the destruction of Israel. It was not a perfect time of God blessing the Jews with apparent prosperity but of rich people exploiting the poor, buying off judges, and selling justice, cheating their customers, corruption, and immorality. At first invasion by the Assyrians, the ten northern tribes escaped and spread to other regions forever, so foreign Assyrians started living in the region with remaining Jews and became the Samaritan people. When the Greek *Alexander the Great invaded Israel*, circa 300 BC, it happened that all major Israel nations were destroyed and was no more a king at Damascus, Philistia, Tyre, Edom, Ammon, Moab, and Judah.

Book 31

Obadiah

Obadiah was a small writer but was enough to pass his *message* in the original Hebraic language. The Edomite Jews were neighbors at the south of Judah and the closed escape site from the north invaders. Obadiah, in his judgement message, treats the Edomite Jews as enemies, by repealing the help to family root people. *A lot was told about Edom and its capital, Petra.* The prophet's message was that the natural defenses of the city to the invaders would not be to God, and the destruction would come as a result of the wrong things done. The people who suffer the most are the orphans, widows, and foreigners, treat them well, because the Jews were foreigners in Egypt, and they did not like to be oppressed. And so it happened—the red stone fortresses fell to the Babylonians by 553 BC.

Book 32

Jonah

The Old Scripture's book that brings the prophetic *message* from *Jonah* is small and controversial and was not written by Jonah. Around 750 BC, Jonah predicted the fall of the city of Nineveh, capital of Assyria.[10] Jonah had a *vision*, and God sent him to Nineveh to advise them and repent of their sins. Jonah didn't attend to God's request. Instead, afraid to be killed there, he departed by boat in the opposite direction, at Mediterranean, and in a storm was thrown out of the boat, *got himself swallowed by a large fish*, survived for three days in the fish's belly until the fish spat him out at the coast. True or story invented as a miracle, he decided then to go to Nineveh, advising the people, and the people believed in Jonah's message, repented of their sins, and the city was not destroyed as in the prediction. Jonah's prophecy from God did not happen. He was frustrated with God.

---

[10] Today, Nineveh is an archeologic place in northern Iraq.

Book 33

Micah

Prophesying the same as *Amos*, Micah lived in the same time, for more than fifty years, and his *message* was religious to God. *Micah predicted* Israel's destruction, gave sentences to powerful legislators, condemned the oppression of the poor, injustice at the courts, and idolatry on created gods. Most of the wrongdoings were from leaders, judges, and richest people. He lived to see the destruction of Samaria and Jerusalem, both countries' capitals, by the Assyrian invasions at around 720 BC in the north and 700 BC in the south. But Micah finished his predictions with a new start, bringing back his exiled people to rebuild the nation and announcing the new leader, as the Messiah, that should be born in Bethlehem.

Book 34

Nahum

Nahum's visions from God were predictions to happen about what Jonah had predicted before, the Assyrian barbarian empire and the idolatry's capital, Nineveh, that oppressed all the enemies' lands with killings and possession, are to be destroyed by the Babylonians one hundred years later.

Book 35

Habakkuk

He was in Judah doing his teachings to the Jews and was asking for God to help him to give direction to Jews' behavior—they were violent and destroying the enemies, as well as doing corruption and injustices to their own people.

The book of prophet *Habakkuk* is a speech with God. His *vision* is about the power of the Babylonians that will come over the sinners. Habakkuk did not like the people's destiny, so he asked God to correct the people and their heresies because the Babylonians, who destroyed the Assyrians, are sinners, killers and will destroy also the Jews. So Habakkuk put his faith in God, and nobody will take possession of it. The prophet was a writer of poems, psalms, and songs, singing religious works for the praise of God.

God's message to him:

Write down what you see and note on signboards to be able to read fluently. Because the vision is still far, but by the end, it will be fulfilled and will not be forgotten; and the just will live in its faith.

Book 36

Zephaniah

Lived at the south of Judah, at the same time as Nahum. *Zephaniah* received the *message* from God in a single phrase, I the Lord, promise to destroy everything in the earth, people and animals, birds and fish, eliminating all the human race. This message was very dramatic and hard to pass on to the people, and only Israel was considered to be punished mainly by the list of sins of the leaders and powerful people.

What happened was the Romans destroyed Jerusalem forty years later but after that brought Jews back from exile to rebuild their nation. "At last your troubles will be over and you will never again fear disaster."

Book 37

Haggai

The Persians recorded the happenings eighteen years after the Jews came back from exile by 500 BC. Then a great drought happened, so *Haggai wrote* what he saw and what the Lord God *messaged* to him about not having a temple for so long. Then Haggai called on the people to rebuild the temple. God blessed the people and the long drought was finished. The new temple was finished by 520 BC.[11] The temple was enlarged by 20 BC by King Erodes, but once more, the temple got destroyed in AD 40 by the Romans.

---

[11] Today what remains is a small part of the wall where the Jews worship religiously.

Book 38

Zechariah

One of *Zechariah's* prophecies was God's message about good things on Jews' behaviors and Jesus's arrival, which was predicted by Isaiah as well.[12] He had at least *eight visions*, which were interpreted to mean that good things were coming, like the construction of the temple and the Greeks defeating the Persians in the famous battle of Marathon. In this occasion, some Greek[13] soldiers ran forty-two kilometers to communicate their victory.

---

[12] Around 500 years before it happened, Zechariah also predicted the coming of Jesus.

[13] The Greeks, in old ages, lived before the Romans, and to survive attacks of the enemies' possession, they fought the people invading from the orient, mainly the Babylonians and Assyrians. But in counterpart, to expand territory, they also invaded the neighbors like the people living in Canaan land, the Jews in the south coast of the Mediterranean Sea, because they need to shore their ships and get across their land to fight their enemies strategically from the back, in their territory.

Book 39

Malachi

He was one of the last of the prophets in his time—with Haggai and Zechariah.[14] *Malachi* warned the Jews to not sacrifice sick animals, not marry women that were practicing idolatry, not treat to the poor badly, and, instead, to serve in the name of God and not to insult him. The Jews stopped the offerings practices but not completely, because at the temple, the Jews were keeping tradition for some ministries. Anyway based in Zechariah prophetic *visions* from God, it was helping in return with protection and crops with abundance. Malachi *previewed* that Jesus would be a *sheep of God* and this was later confirmed by the disciple, John, *the Lamb of God who should remove the sins of the world.*

---

[14] The prophecies on earth were finished, according to Jewish wisdom, in the years that follow. This book of Malachi completes the thirty-nine books of the Old Scriptures.

Covenant between God and People

The Ten Commandments

1. Thou shalt have no other gods before me.
2. Thou shalt not make unto thee any graven image.
3. Thou shalt not take the name of the Lord thy God in vain.
4. Remember the Sabbath day, and keep it holy.
5. Honor thy father and thy mother.
6. Thou shalt not kill.
7. Thou shalt not commit adultery.
8. Thou shalt not steal.
9. Thou shalt not bear false witness against thy neighbor.
10. Thou shalt not covet anything that is thy neighbor's.

Prophets

Visionaries, Dreamers, Predictors

They are the important parts of the Scripture. They have been the communication channel or link between God and the human beings. Mainly in the Old Scriptures, dreams were the advice or alert or teachings provided as compensation for the hard work or way correction and behavior of the people. To be a prophet was to preach God's existence, to support the Jewish believers, and to go against sin, especially idolatry and wrong behavior in making sacrifices. Prophets had to put high efforts for the interpretation, predicting the major catastrophes of their kingdom like the Egyptian king's dream, which Joseph, son of Jacob, foresaw as the plagues, allowing the Jews to travel back to Israel and leave the slavery life.

The meaning of the message had to be premonitory, with precise perception about what is right or fake, with consciousness.

New Scriptures

The New Scriptures started with eleven books in AD 150, but along the studies, the *church leaders of the Christian Church at Carthage Council in AD 397 concluded in twenty-seven books*, beginning with Matthew and ending with the book of Revelation.

Book 1

Matthew

Around 6 BC until AD 30, *Matthew* did write this book telling about the caravans coming from Babylon, journeying to find the promised Messiah that was coming to Israel. The *prophecies* were so strong, since the time of Isaiah and others prophets that three wise magis, Melchior, Balthazar, and Gaspar, grouped in the region of Iraq and Iran to come to Jerusalem to show respect to the birth of the boy who was destined to be a leader. The magi followed a light from a *star* to Bethlehem, and King Herod, knowing this from the magi in 4 BC, sent out orders to authorities to kill all the boys born two years old or less in Bethlehem, so his kingdom would not have another king.

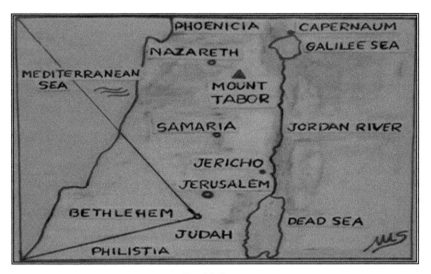

Bethlehem

To escape from King Herod, Joseph went to Egypt. When they returned after Herod had died, Matthew was the Roman king's tax charger. Then it happened that Jesus invited him to join the group of disciples.

The most part of Jesus's teachings had happened in Galilee mountings.

The Jews were frustrated thinking that what was coming was a great warrior king like David, but they got a no-battle person to save the world. Matthew and the others disciples, pointed out that was fulfilled all prophecies, Jesus with the wise teachings and miracles at the spiritual level of salvation, not for one but for all to eternal life.

Matthew did not write about Jesus's first years of life but went directly to the baptism of Jesus by John the Baptist when he was thirty years old, after Jesus's forty days in the desert. At this time, Jesus left Nazareth and went to Capernaum, beside the Sea of Galilee, to the north of Israel. He then seated at the hillside and started giving his disciples a series of speeches (i.e. the Sermon on the Mount). The teachings were directed to the good, correct, and right—different from the others rabbis. When praying say: Our Father who art in heaven, hallowed be Thy name. Thy kingdom come, Thy will be done on earth as it is in heaven, give us this day our daily bread, and forgive us our trespasses as we forgive those who trespass against us, and lead us not into temptation, but deliver us from evil.

The people followed Jesus after his teachings and then it happened—the miracle of the multiplication of the two fishes and five loaves. During the three years of teachings of Jesus, he assigned Simon, naming him Peter, to be the leader of the disciples, and he assigned him the construction of the Christian church. After Jesus's death, resurrection, and ascension, *Peter performed the first sermon in Jerusalem*, in a reunion of more than 3,000 Jews, which became the first large conversion and *foundation of the Catholic Church*.[15] At the week of the crucifixion, Jesus reunited with the disciples and commemorated the Jews' Passover from the Egypt Exodus, and this became the Last Supper with the bread and wine symbolically as his body and blood.

Matthew's book describes all the final passages of Jesus—from being judged by the Jewish leader, Caiaphas, and being buried by Pilate's Roman soldiers. At the end, on Easter Sunday, Mary Magdalene, Mary (mother of James), and Salome went to the tomb and knew what happened—the resurrection of Jesus Christ.

---

[15] Two historical places are set until today—near the Galilee Lake, the first Church of Peter, and over Mount Tabor, the Transfiguration Church, built about AD 400 after the legalization of Christianity.

Book 2

Mark

Mark's source of information was Peter and elapsed three years of Jesus's teachings. Simon (Peter) and Andrew (see pictures below) were fishermen, and Jesus offered to them to be fishers of men if they follow him. Along the Galilee Lake, they met James and John and with the same proposal, they followed him. Andrew listened from John the Baptist who said that Jesus was the *Lamb of God who removes the sins of the world*. To his disciples, Jesus asked, "And you, whom do you say I am?" Answering, Peter said, *"You are the Christ, the Messiah."*

Jesus settled in Capernaum, and there he chose Mathew, another disciple. He was the Romans' tax collector. The same way following invitations, started grouping the twelve, been all simple men.

As the Messiah Jesus turned all previous Jews' concepts, no sacrifices, with miracles[16] and teachings by example[17] and tasks in the Jews Sabbath. The Jews wanted a king that would free them from the Romans, and Jesus, till the last moment, affirmed, *"My Kingdom is not from this world."* Jesus passed God's message for everybody salvation to all his followers, and compared us to the smallest seed, it depends of the ground were flourishes, as well as the children are the pureness model for heavens kingdom.

Jesus starting a group of disciples

---

[16] *The ten most important miracles* in the scriptures: 1-*Rasing dead Lazarus (John)*, 2-Walking on the water (Mark), 3-Feeding around 5,000 people (Mark), 4-Transforming water into good wine (John), 5-Calming a storm (Mark), 6-Healing a Roman officer's servant (Matthew), 7-Healing a bleeding woman (Mark), *8-Healing a man born blind (John)*, 9-Healing a paralyzed man (Mark), 10-Whithering a fig tree (Mark).

[17] *The ten most important parables*: 1-The good Samaritan (Luke), 2-*The prodigal son (Luke)*, 3-The lost sheep (Matthew), 4-Farmer planting seeds (Mark), 5-The mustard seeds (Mark), 6-The ten virgins at a wedding (Matthew), 7-The lost coin (Luke), 8-Three servants with investment money (Matthew), 9-The back/last seat at the party (Luke), 10-The rich man and Lazarus (Luke).

To the twelve apostles, Jesus passed instructions to go and seek the lost sheep from the house of Israel. To do this task to spread my word, take care of yourselves, because for my cause you will be taken to governors and kings as witness to them, to speak at that hour, will be inspired what to say, because will not be you speaking, but the Spirit of the Father speaking in you.

Book 3

Luke

The book from a man called Luke is the history of the Christian religion, written in letters by the time of the execution of Paul in Rome. Since Luke was a friend of Paul in many of Paul's trips, he compounded the letters and delivered to an official Roman named Theophilus, with the purpose of defending Paul. Paul preached the teachings of Jesus and treated *Jesus's history as a Savior, the Christ* (*Messiah* in Jewish). The history told from the year 6 BC through AD 30 was written till before Paul's execution at around years AD 60 when the gospel spread to the Roman Empire, since Jesus teachings to the apostles, telling about Him to spread the word to all, to the ends of the earth, as Luke wrote also in his book Acts of the Apostles.

Jesus was born in Bethlehem, at the south of Jerusalem, but the family was living more than one hundred kilometers in Nazareth, at the north of Israel, but because the Roman Emperor, Augustus, planned to make a general census then all the families should go to their descendants' cities. When he was twelve years of age, at the commemoration of the Passover, the annual day of Jews' return from Egypt, Jesus went from Nazareth to Jerusalem with the family. Showed to be a special boy, he left his parents, Joseph and Mary, stayed at the Jewish temple, and started talking about religion with the religious rabbis, communicating with them with prodigious insights. His mom searched for him and upon having found him, he justified to his mom, "I have a mission to accomplish, *didn't you know that I must be in my Father's house.*'"

Jesus, as a rabbi, was established at Capernaum village, beside the lake region at the Galilee. He had gathered fame in performing miracles and sapient teaching but with new ideas. He went to Nazareth, his hometown as a child, a daylong trip from Capernaum, for the religious event in the synagogue. During the ritual services, like a mass, the reading was from the Prophet Isaiah—that God's messenger, a Messiah, was to come to bring the good news to the needy people, to look on freedom on doing the right, to make the blind see, to give the oppressed their freedom. *In response to the readings from the Prophet Isaiah, Jesus said that he was him, the Messiah of the scriptures,* that was said seven hundred years ago. The worshippers almost stoned him in disbelief to his powers, but he escaped and returned to Capernaum. From this time on, Jesus did more miracles to show his special powers of healing and helping the people. With his wisdom, he taught by parables showing that one must do the good to have the reward for the good coming from God, the Creator.

Luke wrote about the crucifixion and death of Jesus as Matthew did. Pilate, knowing that Herod's son, the governor of Nazareth, Herod Antipas, is in Jerusalem, sends Jesus to him to sentence him for claiming that he was the Messiah, son of God. Antipas sends him back to Pilate, who is convinced by the Jewish council that he should be crucified.

Book 4

John

He probably wrote his book after Matthew, Mark, and Luke and has probably read their writings since for writing, he searched for the *signs that most demonstrated Jesus as the son of God.* From the seven miracles shown, the most important was the resurrection of Lazarus three days after his death. It was the most shocking at that time—showing that he had power even over death, the limitations of people and things. The prophets had already announced that the Messiah should open the blinds eyes. *John* did not repeat a lot of things from the other disciples but said more about cases and teaching histories of Jesus—*if everybody believes him, they will have the eternal life.*

For him, raising his eyes, Jesus said, Father, the hour has come, glorify your Son, that the Son may glorify the Father, even as you gave Him authority over all mankind, that to all whom the Father has given Him, He may give eternal life. And this is eternal life that they may know the Father, the only true God, and Jesus Christ whom the Father has sent. I glorified the Father on the earth, having accomplished the work which you have given Me to do.

John described Jesus as *the Word, the Word was with God, and the Word was God.*[18] Other statement with several meaning was calling Jesus the bread of life. At one occasion, Jesus stayed overnight in Jerusalem, went to Nicodemus's house who was one of the most influential Jewish leaders who had the power to create and apply laws. *Nicodemus said to Jesus, "Your miracles signs, are evidences that God is with you."*

The Last Supper

---

[18] Scholars estimate that the Christian writings from John were done in a decade around AD 80, and that, it summarizes his witness to Jesus's life.

Book 5

Acts of the Apostles

When the ascension of Jesus happened, the disciples replaced Judas Iscariot by Matthias, becoming twelve again. They returned to Jerusalem and gathered, about one hundred twenty followers (included in this group are all their brothers and Mary, his mother), when *tongues of fire appeared from the sky and fell over each of them, and to them, signs of wisdom started to be evident*—they could speak other languages. In this day is commemorated the *creation of the Christian religion*. Peter made his first speech that Jesus had resurrected, and he was going to spread the truth to all believers, and to him joined 3,000 people and were baptized and integrated to the church that day, most if not all were Jews. The scenery, as the time passed, was that in all Mediterranean, the good news was spread to all Roman Empire by the next thirty to forty years.

The Acts of the Apostles, attributed to *Luke*, tells about what happened to Jesus after he left this planet. When Jesus's last talk to the disciples happened, it was to return to Jerusalem and *wait for the Holy Spirit*, and he was going to the One who sent him. The encourager was coming. He spoke about the Holy Spirit that was coming over them, and they would be his witnesses, telling about him in Jerusalem, in Judea, in Samaria, and to all the earth.

Peter and John were put in jail after preaching the word of Jesus, but because of fear of a riot by the Jews against the Romans, they were released with the condition that they were never to teach about Jesus. However, that never happened. Instead, more and more became followers of Christ,[19] but many of those converted were persecuted or killed, but the rich and poor joined together in movement—the rich sold their properties to help the poor followers to survive. Meanwhile a follower, named Stephen, faced the religious Jews leaders, justifying that they were against God, that even the scriptures were telling that the Messiah would arrive and, as in the scriptures, that they did sacrifice him in the cross. The Jews that judged Jesus concurred to have him stoned to death. Saul (Paul in Greek) saw this execution; he has no mercy, being a cruel Jew, and believes that other Jews, like Stephen who is spreading wrong religious practices, must be jailed and judged. There's a branch of Judaism believers that believe Jesus is the divine son of God, the way, the truth, and the life. The movement was called *The Way*. Saul (Paul), five years after Jesus's death, left in persecution to these followers in Damascus, but reaching near the city, a mysterious light blinded him. He fell to the ground, then a voice called him, "Saul, Saul! Why are you persecuting me?"

"Who are you?" asked Saul.

"I am Jesus. The one you are persecuting! Now stand up, and go to the city, and you will receive instructions for what you need to do."

Once in the city, a man called Ananias who was a follower of the Christian movement, The Way, had a vision instructing him to convert Saul. Ananias resisted because he knew about

---

[19] Countless interpretations were raised by groups or followers. The Jews were still followers of the old rules of sacrifices and practices not worshipped by Jesus, like circumcision, the animal's food, the commerce of things not Christians, of idolatries and sacrifices.

Saul's authority, that Saul could put him in jail. But the message of the vision was clear, *Saul is my instrument in taking my message to all the people or kings.* Ananias converted Saul, and he changed his name to Paul to join the followers, telling his fantastic transformation and the good news about Jesus.[20]

The disciples had so much conviction of the eternal life by doing Jesus's cause that were not giving attention of the danger about their life, during their teachings left by Jesus and so they went to the people.

The Acts of the Apostles records the causes of deaths of almost all martyrs who have been Jesus's messengers. It was by their faith that they risked their life to the persecutors. *This way was James, by the sword of King Herod; Peter and his brother, Andrew, crucified in Rome; Philip, crucified in Turkey;* Bartholomew, behead in India; Thomas, after starting several churches in India, also beheaded in India; Matthew, by the sword in Ethiopia; James, son of Alpheus, crucified in Egypt; Thaddaeus, son of James, with Simon the Zealot, martyred in Iran; Matthias, stoned and beheaded; John, brother of James, the only natural death in Ephesus in Turkey; the preachers disciples were Paul, Luke, Mark, and Matthew, only tens of years after that, the Christianity was authorized by Rome.

With the teachings of Jesus, one by one, the solutions solved by Paul and his missionaries, but even so Paul was not spared; he was jailed and judged by the Roman Emperor, Caesar, around the end of AD 60, came out in history to have been executed or without known end.

---

[20] Paul traveled in missionary expedition at least three times in twenty years, between Jerusalem and Greece, without counting his expedition in Rome in AD 59. *Paul created at least twenty churches* in Turkey, Cyprus, Greece, and Syria.

Book 6

Romans

Paul was meeting with Christians in Greece, doing missionary work and writing letters to the Roman Christians that he knew as friends for long time and are Christian believers. The Roman Empire was extending to the coastlands of Mediterranean, and there were millions of souls to do missionary work, so Paul that passed twenty years in the east, now writes that have intensions to go till Spain to the west and after that stop to travel.

Three years later, he went to Rome for his trial. In Rome, Paul wrote the most eloquent book about Christianity—about the world's creation, the physical universe, that it was *impossible for something to come out from nothing*. Paul then stated that may have more than one physical dimension to create and keep the universe evolution. Unfortunately, sinners take God out of this equation and make weak theories about God, so the sins, anger, hate, murder, frustration, bad behavior, gossip, and envy fill up their lives. Also, a person without religion who doesn't know about the Ten Commandments could show that he knows the law *because he fulfills them by instinct*, even though he has never heard of them before. The laws of God are in their hearts and consciousness, showing what is right. The secret life of each one will not be hidden to God and his son, Jesus Christ. The faith and then the obedience determine our eternal destiny.[21] I find, though, this law in myself:

> When I want to do the well, the evil is close to me, because I have praise in Gods' law, according to a man interior, but I see in my members other law that opposes to my spirit law, and make me slave of the sin law, that is in my members. Sadness to myself! Who will make me free of this body of death? Only by Gods' grace by Jesus Christ our Lord. So, though, I obey to God with my spirit; and please the sin law with my flesh.

Paul says, speaking to those followers suffering with sins: I love God over all the others things, but there is another power in me that is in war with my thoughts. It is thought over material; sacred thoughts over sinful things. The choice is yours. Leave yourself to be commanded by sacred spirit and will be given the eternal live. Paul compares this with a person walking on a mountain. On the way, the sin pulls one down whereas the good pulls up, but it is a lot easier to go down.

A lot of people who read the letter to the Romans changed their lives.

---

[21] If the faith is a chicken and good things are the eggs, then the chicken comes first, so will be crossing the street to go to heaven.

Books 7–8

Corinthians 1 and 2

Paul wrote letters to the Corinthians to solve their doubts on faith and procedures of the Jewish law, which was dividing its church and the teaching done during his missionary trips. He addressed the matters pertaining circumcision, sexuality and incest, mass ritual, communion, behavior of women speaking during the mass, and so on.

To bond all together, Paul says that spiritual gifts are temporary and will be intended to drive you to Christ. It deals with three particular features that *stays forever—faith, hope, and love.*

Paul told the Corinthians about all the people who saw Jesus, counting more than five hundred of them. If disciples and witnesses can lie and Paul took the following explanation about the resurrection, this is the good news about Christianity. If Christ did not resurrect, then your faith is useless and you are still guilty for your sins. In this case all the people that are dead believing in Christ are lost! And if our hope in Christ is only for this life, we are more merciful then any one other in this world.

In one of his teachings, in one of his letters, Paul talks about the contributions that he needed for the *poor Christians in Jerusalem*—he needed the donations generously sent from the non-Jewish part of the church; this would help the Christian Jews to accept them, unifying the church. The charity is patience, beneficial, is not envious, nothing to be afraid of, and now remains for us the faith, hope and charity the most important. But this didn't work, arriving in Jerusalem with the donations, he was jailed for several years and ending up being sent to Rome to be judged. He was released, but years later, he was put to jail again and executed.

Book 9

Galatians

Faith in Jesus is the only thing that can save us and not merely the compliance to Jewish rules like the circumcision and special food to be eaten in Jewish manner.

At this subject, Paul disagreed with Peter when in an occasion, Peter was visiting the churches that Paul had founded. Peter was treating the local Christians normally, visiting and eating with them, but when the Jews showed up to state their point about their rules, he turned his back to the local non-Jews. The book to the Galatians (today Turkey) that *Paul* wrote in approximately AD 50 is a lesson to Peter about *not denying what Jesus preached with the Gentiles,* non-Jews, accepting the Christianity's freedom preached by Jesus's good news. Being a Christian is to live in communion with the saintly Spirit. The laws were our guardian until when the faith in Christ came, the same faith in God, blessed in Abraham.

Book 10

Ephesians

The letter written by *Paul* to the Ephesians in around the AD 60. The region had a solid Christian basis and acceptance, confirming the point of living the life full with love and following Christ's example. The teachings to us is to be doing all efforts for keeping people united in one only Spirit and looking for peace. Paul stayed some years in Ephesus, one of the bigger cities of the Roman Empire, headed by Rome and Alexandria in Egypt. Paul preached that the non-Jew Christians were included in the salvation taught by Christ and that the *commandments and Abraham's rules were obsolete* because *the death of Jesus* in the cross was for forgiveness of our sins that *was a step ahead of God in the salvation plan.*

According to Paul, we can know our physical measures, but how can we measure our spirit? How can we have the dimension of the maturity of our faith? For us to keep in the way, Paul wrote a list of good behaviors and actions. Paul wrote about the families, husband and wife, children, slaves and superiors, clamming for yourself, and respect in all relationship. The healthy family did not stay around the argument of who is in command but obeys the new teaching provided by Jesus, "Love one another."

Book 11

Philippians

The Philippi city is located in Greece, but the letter to the Philippians from *Paul* was written when he was in jail under the Roman guards in some Roman cities—Rome, Caesarea, Ephesus, or Corinth. The Philippians sent clothes, money, and food to Paul to whom he was thankful for, for their generosity and to whom he advised to keep the Christianity. The city had great geological richness and was developed by the Macedonian king; it was the Philippi King father of Alexander the Great that gave the name of the city. Paul, during the second trip, *founded in the city his first church congregation*, at the region of European continent. In AD 64, Rome was on fire, and Nero blamed the Christians to have started the destruction. Nero started the persecution to the Christians, and 11,000 were out to death in the Roman Coliseum and all the empire's territory. With the strength of faith and the promise of salvation, holding on to the eternal life promised by Christ, the Christians did not fear death. Paul, knowing about the competitions in Olympia in Greece, illustrated that by known events to compare and pass the message, they should run for a great prize, We do it for the eternal life in heaven.

Book 12

Colossians

The letter to the Colossians, was written by *Paul* to help the church minister in Colossae who reported to have problems with the followers,[22] with religious behavior: spiritual-over-material. Also, it was hard for the non-Jews to have to follow Jewish rules for the salvation. The people's practices in Colossae is a confusing belief of Jewish teachings, gnostic, astrology, and evil spirits. Paul insisted that once you accept Jesus Christ as your Lord, you must continue to follow him, *Let your roots grow deep in Him* and your life be built in Him. Don't let someone trap you with empty statements and not well defined.

Paul's short letter finished with a listing of good practices for the Christian followers, avoid the luxury, immorality, dirty language, pursuing kindness things, generosity, and forgiveness to who is offending, gentleness and in this way have unity on Christian church behavior.

---

[22] This letter, as the others, was written in the prison, telling the Christians that they should consider old sinful lives as dead and gone.

Books 13–14

Thessalonians 1 and 2

In his second trip, going with Silas, *Paul* passed by Turkey and went to Greece, passed by Thessalonica and preached to non-Jews and Jews, converting many people, passed by Athens and went to Corinth. Then he got news about the problems of the church's new believers in Thessalonica, but he knew he couldn't return, so he started communicating his teachings through letters.

Based on what Paul said, the church seemed to have three main questions: What to do with the persecution that they live; *how should the Christians behave?* When is Jesus coming? What happened to the Christians who died before?

Thessalonica was a large free city of the empire, located along Roman Egnatian way, linking all the orient to Rome—passing soldiers, merchants, and travelers.[23] The challenge was to stop the commerce of the idols and its profits, changing to believe in Jesus and in one universal God. Paul was a Jew and believes in what Jesus preached to the Jews, believes in the good news behavior with the Holy Spirit to drive the people to the

---

[23] Today in the region of Thessaloniki, there are more than three hundred churches that were started since AD 300, all of them in Paul's intentions and his ministry.

eternity, since when the apostles were blessed with the Holy Spirit in Jerusalem. Paul did introduce the message of Jesus in synagogues initially, and many rabbis were participating, but what made it harder was his message was sounding to be from one religious sinner. Paul tried to take the Thessalonica Jews, for only three weeks, to the old Jewish scriptures, showing that the life and ministry of a Messiah was predicted, but they didn't understand that God had a Son, even with all the miracles he did, and this was already twenty years after Jesus's resurrection. They wanted to kill Paul, and he had to escape, persecuting till the next city. He escaped again to Corinth, and for this, Thessalonica was persecuting all the followers of the locals good news movement. *To the Thessalonians, reaching spiritual maturity* was what Paul desired. We all make mistakes, but we do not choose sin over what we know God wants us to do. God wants us to grow from the spiritual infant to the strong adult spirituality.

Books 15–16

Timothy 1 and 2

The letter from *Paul* to his colleague, Timothy,[24] was written in some place at the North Greece to Ephesus in the Turkish side, where Timothy was his designated representative for the local church. It took a few years of work to establish the church there, but some problems were left for Timothy to solve. So Paul wrote, Live and teach the opposite to the hungry for money Christians. God's people need to be rich in good work and generosity to whom is in necessity. This way will be saving a treasure with good foundation to the future and experiencing the true life.

For the church's leaders, Paul gave a special recommendation to Timothy: the elderly leader must exercise the auto-control, live wisely, and have a good reputation.

In his second letter, written around AD 67, Paul called Timothy to Rome, dramatically waiting for the execution as a result of the emperor's judgment. He needed to give to him the last request: Do not have fear. Come stay with me. The persecution that he was having was going to be extended to all the empire, and he would give up on the faith. Remember that *Jesus*

---

[24] Timothy's parents were non-Jews.

Christ resurrected from death; this is what I minister to everyone.[25] If we die with Him, we also live with Him, if we resist with Him, we reign with Him. Gentle teach to those that resist to the true, may be God changes the people's hearts.

---

[25] Timothy became the bishop in Ephesus, martyrized in AD 97.

Book 17

Titus

Titus was living in the Crete Island in the south of Greece. He was *Paul's* disciple, and a letter was written to him, similar to the letter sent to Timothy. Paul knew that Crete's people were originated from people without laws and country, pirates and cruel, so Titus was going through a lot of difficulties, but Paul knew that this people (even though spiritually sick) are the ones who needed Jesus the most. Titus was selecting leaders for the church in the middle of people who were rough, liars, and lazy gluttons. All the basics of the good behavior written to Timothy were passed to Titus. Paul wanted Christianity to be trans-formed in a shining light of the Roman Empire, *the spiritual power for the good in an evil world.*

Book 18

Philemon

He was the leader of the Christian congregation that was doing reunions at his house in Colossae, when his slave Onesimus ran away and met *Paul* and he was converted. This happened probably in Rome, at the time Paul was waiting for his judgment. Paul requested Onesimus to return to his owner. Paul wrote a letter to Philemon to release Onesimus and send him back to him. Paul believed that Christians should treat all kinds of people with respect and love as one would treat oneself. When Christians would start doing this, owners would become servers, and slaves would get human freedom to work for servers. His letter was convincing, full of humanitarian reasons, and had a gentle approach. Paul said that Onesimus became his son in faith, treated him with love. He said, "He wants to work with me, but I am sending him back to you. To have your allowance. He no longer is a slave, he is more than a slave because he is a loved brother."

Book 19

Hebrews

The prophet Isaiah announced in 800 BC that when the Messiah was coming, should have a new beginning. In the book written by the *Hebrews*, is highlighted that the Jewish religion based in the rules and rituals would be past dated, should be replaced by the Christian practices and Jesus's sacrifice to all.

By the years AD 40 to 70, the Romans demolished the Jewish temple in Jerusalem, ending this way the animals offerings in sacrifice. Mainly to the Jewish-Christians, how to reach to God to have mercy and seek forgiveness of their sins, everything was changing because now they should follow Jesus, the Messiah, as announced and predicted in the old scriptures.

Emperor Constantine legalized Christianity in AD 313 and a few years later became the official religion in all the Roman Empire. Jesus, by his sacrifice, has forever released the people from sins. *No more sacrifices, forget the past sins, no more be slave of the sins*, in place was liberty. Liberty of rituals, liberty of praising God, liberty serving God to receive the requested mercy because the sacrifice was done by Jesus's death on the cross. The Hebrews writer want us to remember that faith is more important to God than the rituals. Remember self who teach the God's words which came to your life and listen to the example of your faith. Jesus Christ is the same, yesterday, today and forever.

Book 20

Thiago

He was son of Zebedee who was an important person in Jerusalem's religious community. Thiago was a cousin of Jesus. *Thiago* wrote this letter because he was the leader of the Christian Jews until about AD 60. He preached the following: to have control about what was talked, that a little thing from the tongue can take your life to the fire, to not give preferences to the richness, and to treat the hard times as opportunities to grow spiritually. God blesses those who patiently endure testing and temptation.

Thiago's letter called for prophet Job who spoke in name of Lord and showed great endurance. At that time, there was a controversy that richness God's way of blessing his people and that poverty was God's way of punishing.

Thiago preached that *Christians must love all their neighbors, the rich and the poor,* as well as doing examples, "*If you have faith show it by actions this way it's true.*"

Books 21–22

Peter 1 and 2

Nero died in AD 68. The Romans finished the destruction of Jerusalem to the ground in AD 70. For Christianity, it produced a radical change that even the neighbors did not recognizing. *Peter described that this is almost as having been born again.* The non-Jews were participating on festivities and idolatry with several of general gods, but with the conversion to Christianity, they turned to be antisocial and worshipped one Lord. Peter encouraged that life on earth was temporary, and doing this, they were citizens of Heaven.

The letters of *Peter* were sent to the Christians who lived in Asia Minor,[26] all cities where Paul ministered the good news for surviving the religious separations and differences. The first letter was written with the help of Silas in about AD 60 when the Emperor Nero persecuted the Christians because of allegations that the Christians put fire in Rome in July of AD 64. Peter repeated things that Paul taught in all that region—being honorable, not behaving with hypocrisy and jealousy, having a humble attitude, not retaliating with insult to whoever insults you, and respecting the authorities even if they are being cruel.

---

[26] East of Greece, today's Turkey.

With regard to marriage, behave as partners, not slaves and property. In his first worshiping after the resurrection of Jesus, he converted more than three thousand Jews.[27] He died a martyr in Rome; he was crucified.[28]

Before his death, he wrote his last recommendation to *growing in faith*. Do not let that false teachers, leaders or prophets be taken you away from God. Do not be frustrated if Christ has not returned yet. God is patient, for God that exist since before of our physical time have started, a day can be one thousand years, the time can be so compressed in the spiritual life. Do not stay waiting as Peter said. Instead, gives your maximus to be found in your best, in purity and peace.

---

[27] Peter was considered the first Pope, but before that, he was called the Vicar of Christ, bishop of Rome.

[28] He asked to be hung head down.

Books 23–25

John 1, 2, and 3

When John became an older man, he moved to Ephesus in Turkey, and there he wrote the book of Revelation. Many groups have abandoned the churches in the region. John tells that there were those who never truly have been Christians, as they were thinking that everything that comes from the physical body is bad and everything that is spiritual is good. So these people were doing things separately and living in a bad manner, searching for money, sex, and power. *John wrote to them, telling that the authentic Christians live in morality, treating others with love, resisting the temptation of egoism.* About sins, *John wrote that all the sins can be forgiven,* even the mysterious sins that take us to death. *If we ask mercy confessing our sins to Him,* it will be merciful and just forgiving the sins and to cleanse us from all vicious badness.

God made a salvation plan for us, starting with Abraham, a just and righteous man. He chose Israel because, at that time, it was a correct nation. But later on, Israel deviated its destiny and failed to God. So God sent his Son to carry out its mission, so Jesus started presenting to the people how to live as citizens of God's kingdom and he *sent disciples to go and make disciples in all the nations.* In his second letter, John wrote to a church in special, calling it the chosen lady and her children, so his letter could reach to its destination.

John, the older brother of James, knew about a pastor with the name Diotrephes, liked to be leader but used to treat everybody on the manner of not giving even water, food, or lodging for the travelers, mainly to the Christian ministers—*At that desert region, it could mean survival or death to the travelers.* John died after AD 90 and wrote his last letter to a man named Gaius living in the region where Diotrephes lives, on the west coast of Asia. He sent it by a courier named Demetrius, saying that it is blessed by God who helps the passing travelers.

Book 26

Jude

He was a leader of the Christian church in Jerusalem and wrote his letter around the AD 60. His writings matched Peter's ideas at that time. Some Christian scholars started to teach the practices of a Christianity version, the wrong way making doubts about Christ's teachings, satisfying their physical desires, bragging that this was not sin, so *Jude*, as one of the Jesus's brothers reminded the people about the old Jewish writings and teachings, about the destruction of Jerusalem and the exile of the people by about fifty years in Babylon. Cain, who killed his brother, was sentenced to live wandering on the earth without nothing. Sodom and Gomorrah, the cities living in sin, were destructed with its people without any sign in the planet. Jude requested his *followers to stay in true faith* and show mercy for those attracted by the false teachers.

Book 27

Revelation

The heaven and the physical universe do not have relation because heaven is a spiritual place. Spiritual things do not have galactic address. *John*, the apostle, possibly in jail in an island called Patmos in the Asia Minor coast, saw cosmic changes developing in a series of visions that he carelessly wrote. As instructed: Write down all that you see[29] in seven letters and send them to seven churches in the region. *His vision is of a celestial place* where God is worshiped. Someone he described as a Lamb that has been martyrized, presumed to be Jesus, started to unroll a scroll with seven seals; each one when broken seemed to open a window, letting John see future disasters. Wars, famine, and diseases which wiped out part of the humanity. Christians were martyred for their religion. A massive earthquake shook the planet; the fall of stars transformed the planet back to the Stone

---

[29] There are several genres in the writing of scriptures; in this case, the book of Revelation is apocalyptic (Greek)—in general, to code the writings, avoiding the enemies to use them for persecuting them. This genre was also used by Ezequiel and Daniel during their exiles, but a writer named Zoroaster in Moses times had already used this style of writing; speaking that the good gods are defeating the bad gods, giving hope to their followers for win on the bad times.

Age, driving the people to hide back in caves. John saw good things also—to those that died as martyrs, the heaven became a place without death, pain, cries, or sadness. Satan was defeated, and his followers were pitched into a lake of fire.

God is love.[30] Even when he punishes, he searches to look for redemption: to help the people. He uses the punishment to correct the people—driving far away from evil and the destruction that it causes. Adam and Eve have eaten the fruit from the forbidden tree. This disobedience, in some way, contaminated God's creation,[31] introducing sin and death in the cosmic equation. So *trees of life* sprout up as told along the scriptures—from Genesis to Revelation is the history of God working his plan to correct the damage.

---

[30] According to scholars, the book is full of symbolism: God in his goodness wins. Satan and evil lose. *The bad times for the Christians*, perhaps, should be during the persecution of the Roman Emperor Domitian from his reigning time in AD 80 to 90.

[31] In the manifestation of Jesus Christ, most people believe that there are two stages of life: The first is self-orientation—concerned by achievements, success, marriage. The second stage of life, perhaps around age 40 to 45, is what gives meaning to our life—no longer doing the old pleasures that just don't satisfy. Because desire and passions are seen as causes of unhappiness, we are never satisfied and never will be, but God changes the course of the events. God speaks to us.

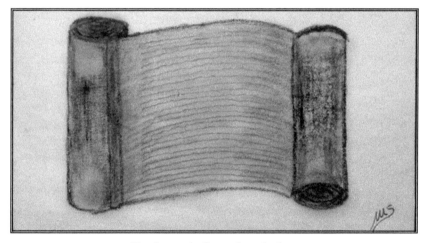

Book, made from sheep's skin

Statements

1. Our destiny is to go to paradise or something nice.
   The end of all subjects leads us to the conclusion that the world is all connected. This is true. There's a reason to live on top of all the things that happen on earth.
   If it is not true, you are doing something wrong, and you admit to be going to other place.
2. Who is in control of your life?
   If the response is you, you need to explain all things that happen in the world and affect your life at the end. On the other hand, all the things that you do affect the other people, too, so you are affecting others. The conclusion is that above all of us, somebody is in control.
3. On passing by a church, visit it.
   When in front of heaven's door, God will recognize you.
   Go to church once a week to give thanks and pray. Pray for the next week to be good for humanity, as good as it was on the past week.
4. Your life is your house.
   Imagine Jesus knocking in your front door. You open the door and show the rooms to him. Now there is a room that is closed. There are your secrets, sins, actions—open that room too.

5. From millennials until now, only one event showed the possibility of an existing human spiritual powers on earth—the resurrection of Jesus.

   Conclusion: Civilizations before the rising of Jesus were never wrong about it.

Prayer

Lord Jesus, I give you all my sins, my addictions, my lust, my greed, all my imperfections, my selfishness, and my weaknesses.

Come and heal the wounds of sin in my life.

Forgive me for all the times I have turned away from your love.

I turn back to you now.

I want to receive your love, your mercy, your forgiveness.

Jesus, I believe that you died to take away my sins.

I believe you are the Christ, the Savior of the world.

I believe in you. I trust in you.

I want to walk with you every day of my life.

I now thank you for healing me. I will follow you always.

Lord Jesus Christ, Son of the living God, have mercy on me a sinner.

Chronological Events

Years Before Christ (BC)

2350—Abraham was born and lived in Ur, a city in the Garden of Eden.

2000—Job, one hundred forty years old, with God, understood the meaning of life.

1800—Joseph, grandson of Abraham, son of Jacob, living in Canaan.

1350—Moses started moving the people back to Canaan.

1349—Moses, after one year from Egypt, camped in Mount Sinai.

1309—Moses camped for forty years in Edom, east side of Jordan River.

1250—Joshua invaded Canaan; people returned to Canaan.

1200—Joshua lives one hundred ten years old; Israel existed again.

1150—David, a young pastor, defeated Goliath; battles all over.

1000—David, a king, expanded Israel's territory; Samson became a myth.

950—Solomon became king.

780—Amos, the prophet, had a vision about Israel's destruction which, indeed, happened as donc by Alexander the Great in around 300 BC.

753—Rome was founded and became an empire.

722—Assyrians destroyed Israel on the north side.

700—Isaiah announced that when the Messiah will come, they should have a new scriptures order.

586—Babylonians destroyed Israel on the south, exiling survivals in Babylon for fifty years.

300—Alexander the Great invaded the Israeli nations, destroying the major kingdoms.

5—Jesus is born around this year, time defined by the year that Rome was founded and the month and year that Herod I (Herod the Great) dies.

Years (AD) Anno Domini

12—Jesus went to the Jewish temple to talk with rabbis and priests.

28—Jesus started to talk and act as the son of God.

30—Estimated time of the execution of Jesus.

59—Paul created at least twenty Christian churches in Turkey, Cyprus, Greece, and Syria.

68—Paul was judged by the Roman Emperor Caesar.

70—The Romans finished to destroy Jerusalem and the temple was brought to the ground by Titus.

80—The gospel spread to all the Roman Empire.

81—Roman Emperor Domitian reined; it was a bad time for the Christians.

313—Roman Emperor Constantine legalized Christianity.

323—Christianity became the official religion in all the Roman Empire.

397—Christian church leaders at Carthage Council concluded twenty-seven books for the New Scriptures.

400—Tabor Mount, Jesus's Transfiguration Church was built.

476—The fall of the Roman Empire happened.

References

Movie References

(Year period. *Titles*. Scriptures)
1350 BC. *Exodus: Gods and Kings*. Egypt.
300 BC. *Alexander*.
AD 28. *Mary Magdalene*. Luke.
AD 30. *The Passion of the Christ*. Matthew and Luke.
AD 30. *Risen*. Acts of the Apostles.
AD 35. *Paul, Apostle of Christ*. Saul the soldier.

Reading References

A Bíblia Sagrada. Sociedade Bíblica do Brasil.
Bíblia Sagrada. Gamma Editorial e Gráfica Ltda. Edições
Paulinas.
Bíblia Sagrada. Tipografia da Pia Sociedade Paulista. Edições
Paulinas.

Index

amos/16,

chronicles/10, corinthians/30, colossians/32,

deuteronomy/8, daniel/15, disciples acts/27,

exodus/6, ezra/10, esther/12, ecclesiastes/13, ezekiel/15, ephesians/31,

genesis/5, galatians/31,

hosea/15, habakkuk/18, haggai/19, hebrews/35,

isaiah/13,

joshua/8, judges/8, job/12, jeremiah/14, joel/16, jonah/17, john/26 and 37, jude/38,

kings/9,

leviticus/7, lamentations/14, luke/25,

Micah/18, malachi/20, matthew/21, mark/23,

Numbers/7, nehemiah/11, nahum/18,

obadiah/17,

psalms/12, proverbs/13, philippians/32, philemon/35, peter/36,

ruth/8, romans/29, revelation/39,

samuel/9, songs of songs/13,

Thessalonians/33, timothy/34, titus/35, thiago/36,

zachariah/19, zephaniah

By the Author

Get the Help from This Book at Today's World

This small book is easy to take with you, on some occasions, when doing nothing but standing, waiting, or traveling, fishing, lying in bed or couch, open it at a random page, read it, and have some message for your life's moment.

About the Author

Mario was born in Veranopolis, Rio Grande do Sul, in the southeast state of Brazil.

As a teenager, he was a member of the youth congregation of Mary at their local parish. This gave to him the Christianity roots for life.

He is married and has three children and six grandchildren; this keeps him and his wife busy all year round.

Professionally, he holds a bachelor's degree in mechanical engineering from UFRGS in Porto Alegre, Rio Grande do Sul, and during his student time worked as a trainee at VARIG where he had the opportunity to fly for the first time to Rome at the time of Pope Paul VI. He later moved to work in Embraer, an airplane manufacturing company supporting customers until retirement. This activity enriched his comprehension of origins and beliefs. His focus was to support airline people in the Americas and Europe through time and to help passengers worldwide.

As a retiree, Mario was inspired to write for people to improve their lives—what this book's purpose is about.

CPSIA information can be obtained
at www.ICGtesting.com
Printed in the USA
BVHW021519140222
628969BV00021B/933

9 781638 442660